Bimboland

Erin Taylor

T0027310

Published in the United States by:
Archway Editions,
a division of powerHouse Cultural Entertainment, Inc.
32 Adams Street, Brooklyn, NY 11201

website: www.archwayeditions.us

Daniel Power, CEO
Chris Molnar, Editorial Director
Nicodemus Nicoludis, Managing Editor
Naomi Falk, Editor

Library of Congress Control Number: 2022936000

ISBN 978-1-57687-991-7

Printed by Toppan Leefung

First edition, 2022

10 9 8 7 6 5 4 3 2 1

Interior layout by Nicodemus Nicoludis

Printed and bound in China

ARCHWAY
EDITIONS

Bimboland

Erin Taylor

Archway Editions, Brooklyn, NY

CONTENTS

for Peter Kropotkin and Kathy Acker
my parents

dull little slut

the dull ordinariness of everything is killing me
      even the most taboo has become daily,
            in your face
            sexual criminality sensuality—ideologically
            opposed to everything not seeped in hedonism
                  my tea is hot yet still no one drinks me

     am I not drinkable, digestible?
            will I give you an upset stomach? do you detest me?
    do you detest the way I shake my little ass, do a fake laugh?

        if I can't cum in the revolution then what's the point?
            the dullest little slut in all the world!

    having a permanent zip code really changed things,
            shook things within me,
                all of a sudden I am showing people pics of anal hooks
                over dinner
                all of a sudden I am word vomiting
      things no one wants to hear about like my pain or my anxieties!

           am I not drinkable, digestible,
           can I nourish nothing but my own boredom?

      I want to go upstate just to say "I went upstate"
            I want to be boring in a hot way

touch me, prove me real!

wishful thinking,
that's what you are

all men are clients,
I almost forgot

discussing CSA in
the surveillance state
group chat

there is something better
at the end of this
but I don't expect

to feed chickens with you
impalpable women of the screen
crawling out of your phone,

how chaotically
I want to be real

a bitch in heat

           it is so funny to find myself
fully content
                          it took me a while to realize
                 the direction I was walking—
crowds of shadows of lines of figure drawings
of figure skaters on the pond in the city, the
children fumbling on the cool slip
           brushing against others as we cross the street
           there are thirty other bodies
                    amoebic movement on hot tar,
                    pavement sweltering through
                    there are several dogs in heat in my dreams
                                                   lately
           I question the use in dreams!
desire and panic and fear all in little thought bubbles
above my head

                 familiar hard boiled eggs cracked
           in a diner on the upper west side that I used to love,
                          thinking about walking from this timeline
                 into your timeline

Avoidance Fetish

I love when I keep my window open
I am a woman…ON THE LOOSE!

as I push my undies in his mouth,
I laugh because it's so easy
I break my nail,
it feels like being a martyr
to something greater than myself
I wanna fuck but not be fucked
I wanna be loved without having to love

feeling close to orgasm as I pick out oranges
in the supermarket

I haven't known what it's like to love deeply in a long time,
so much within me archived in other people
yet I couldn't point myself out in a crowd

without remorse

on this fourth day of the intimate nothing
      I am rubbing my clit to feel something or anything,
      to imagine universes forming

            when I was trapped (as I often am)
            the focus ended on everything I avoid in the dark
            of my body, where I hide what scares me most
            that which reminds me of you

and the hands of men, often rough and tired yet never tired enough
to not find me,

            to not have friction and pressure against me and against all the love
                    I want to no longer be purple and blue
                        at the hands of men bloodied

            I want to be loved, deeply and without remorse for a past life

you grab the shovel, I've got the dirt

burying many lives
my own and others
      how silly the optimism
            I cannot help but feel in my chest
I refuse to dismay despite everything pointed
      downward

             I have dissociated enough of my life
          away
I have briefly lived but I have practice in pausing

we are all just crashing through the air until splat, baby

money burning in the streets in the banks
in the cafes in the brick mortar houses
in the subway tracks ash flutters on the
platform money is burning money is burning
a hole in my pocket your pocket your landlord's
pocket my landlord's pocket!
imagine if everyone stopped paying for anything
at all,
       imagine if money trickled down to the streets
       in the same way a disease can

          swallowing dimes, swallowing fifties
      whole cash bundles whole, nobody wants cash
anymore baby!
             it's all about the ethereum,
the stocks crashed twenty times last week and nobody
      could even have sex with strangers or jump
        off buildings to commemorate

when you don't see me

I want impossible things—
        you don't even have to do anything,
I'm throwing a tantrum over attention
            I want to fuck you in an undisclosed
            location and then buy a car
            that neither of us could afford,
                    drive off somewhere
            but we both love to be mirrored too much

                    wouldn't it be so sexy if you took me seriously?
I don't even know what serious is anymore (that's the joke)

            I hate when I'm feeding chickens and it turns out
            I'm feeding ducks

doing ketamine off a cross with the virgin, Madonna

I never expected cruelty from you, my mistake!
      everyone is up in arms about whores lately,
        they cry about decency and exhausting party antics
yet little did they know my party antics are very decent
      and there's nothing more exhausting than
                                  capitalism!

      it's hot to avoid my feelings at the fun party
it's a powerful room of gays and I am standing on a table in a
bisexual mythic fantasy where the ass smashes a cake
      and I believe in the love of my friends passing
           a bag of dreams around a circle in a bar bathroom

      I want to unearth the madonna and invite her to an orgy,
I want to wash her feet—is it even an orgy if you're not unearthing
all of that bible belt guilt? is it even a party if it doesn't become a
      front and center news crisis,
            "Oh no, the whores have gone political!
Oh! no, the whores have sex!"
            I'm sorry to say my inbox is full
            and it's probably never going to be cleared

teach me how to Unknown

carrying all my baggage everywhere
all the time is exhausting!
      I want to be a light baby doll of a human

I wanna fuck you when I'm not fucking you,
               how are you here all of a sudden!

I try to distract myself from my affection for you by
scrolling on twitter
      there's always something inane and fucked up being
      said online,
      listen to Julia Jacklin, sob at my desk

      healing, unpack my parents at my desk

         to take them little by little out of every
         thing I have around me, that
         touches me
when I think of my father, I smoke—I've been chain smoking
      him out of my system and in and out and in out and

I am gagging!
        it's hard to love and even harder to accept love
      I am a woman surrounded by a series of lakes,
         I have drowned and been baptized and exhausted and
you never really know what is going on, do you!

      I didn't! I didn't know for a long time and once I knew I couldn't
        Unknow!

on being fired for being bisexual

jobs are boring!
jobs are homophobic!
jobs are a waste of my time!
                    of my energy!

        the only thing worth doing is kissing,
        and even that is complicated!

                        I like my love with a little bitter,
                        are we going to fuck tonight?
                my whole body
                has always
                taken up so
                much space!

        I love to get fired from my job for being gay
        on national coming out day!

I love to be queer and alive in 2019,
        snorting friendship in the corner of the peep show

I was alive before I sold myself to capitalism,
        I'll be alive for what seems like forever
        and then BAM I am a eulogy!

but we exist and while we exist I want to
        have an orgasm while having fifty grand thrown on me!

then I never want to think about money again! capeesh?

dissociating on niteflirt

I'm trying to feel happy about a lot of things
but instead I am static
stuck

I miss them,
       I don't know who!
it's fun to dissociate
sometimes
and other times
I forget that I have a therapy appointment
because my brain is a big cloud

I tell man number one on the phone to
send me more
money
and he hangs up

I tell man number two that the first time I pissed
on someone I was
a little pee shy
but ultimately have come to love
yellow heated streams

back to dissociation station,
my sims have
a christmas tree and happy family dynamics

there is zero passive aggression in my sims family
there is no incest
there is only protection and safety
happy holidays

to H, who didn't die young

googling "cock and ball torture techniques"
have you noticed all the google image results are ads now?
I've been thinking about you a lot lately
mostly just curious what you've been up to, obsessed with,
thinking about
when you search "parental estrangement" the video results are
all "How To Handle Being Cut Out By Your Child"
"It's Not Always Your Fault"
                              and maybe for some people that is very true
it is possible that children can be vicious, cruel, unforgiving!
      but all I could think about is you finding that and thinking you can
find some sort of soothing balm to my bitter to my cold to my vicious
                  to my cruelty
                              but I don't think that usually, just lately
it's Christmas soon, you know!
my birthday, the lights of the bar just dimmed
            I think you're sixty-two?
            I don't want to know anything about you
            but I know everything about you
            your name based around a possible death
            a morbid body
            there are articles about what to do when your
            estranged parent is dying
            but I can't imagine a world you do not overtake

lust girl

there's very little to be done about lust,
      or so I've been told my whole life

      letting her guide me with the pink light into violet
      away from your arms his arms her arms the arms of
      those who are too weak to carry me

existing with your violence!
        my pain is all in my head so are you

I have conversations with you

      updating you on all my good news

a family dinner away from home

have found myself at the familiar bend,
or is it more jagged, an edge?

    I have cut myself walking around these
    familiar steps, the backs of my ankles
    bleed out here

        I must be careful
        it takes care to be a woman,
  a woman on my own
  with an understanding of my body
               of myself
                  what is a self that is covered in glass?

my body shard!

      I feel this day in my lower back

    I dissociated in the car,
              a witness is terrifying

I want to be messy in solitude
something rooted in fear of abandonment ya di da da—
    it's a beautiful day on my dead end street that I will never escape

          a family dinner, mashed potatoes, corn, broken
   plates for protein
           crunch crunch crunch!

I love having a family! I love to bleed here with you!
here we are at the edge together, has it ever been so marvelously
lonely? has it ever been this gorgeous and gruesome?
no, it hasn't!

can't stop thinking about touching

no one knows how rent is going to get paid
the diplomat buys me a switch,
      so I don't miss out on the universal
      escape, it's important to me to
be a part of something

      lately been thinking about lust in a way
I haven't in a long time

          I used to touch so much!
    I want   do you understand?

                        unsure
there's a lot going on lately,
      I have only begun to grieve

I love to procrastinate my own grief
by masturbating into an oblivion
      would love to see you there maybe
sometime,
      send me a link

      can't stop thinking about touching
hands at a bar
      on the subway pole
          your face in flatiron!

the conflated you / projecting onto the memory
of every time I have ever felt loved
with future intimacy, touching touching touching

other woman

awhile since I've played
    the other woman,

        I know all the lines
        both the ones I'm supposed to say
        the unspoken uncrossables
            but also that's only if there's a heart
            involved
when you're a professional other woman sometimes
        they like to talk about their wife, they want you
        to know she exists

            but when it's a matter of the heart to be the
            other woman is to be a dream, a fantasy,

            untouched by reality—pure in sin
            a laugh in all things holy
a form of praying when you text me
        "you're all I can think about"
            and niceties about filling me with cum

        I have known how to siren men to disaster
            all my life,
            I always fly close to the sun

sexual liberation is a lie, send tweet

forcing myself to be a fruit of the perfect age
made for eating

I am all juiced up and waiting for you (or anyone)
to place me in your mouth, cut me down with your teeth,
juice running down your face

how do I pick myself off the tree, fresh and wanting,
instead of new hands, with all their grime,
on my peached skin?

I will not always be this young and wet yet I do not
owe this youth to anyone

after labor

I have a full day of doing nothing to look forward to
    I don't believe in a "work culture" because it implies
    a belief in "work"
        a belief in capital, a subtle justification
        of poverty of wealth of cops

        if I ever work in a coworking space, shoot me!
            I want to find a dynamic solution to the end of
            everything we know right now

after therapy I went to the earth room and thought of
a world after us

        a world where every dollar bill is turned into mulch
        and every home overgrown

exhibition champ remorse

find myself in familiar destructive horniness,
that eviscerates the senses

        almost like a sunny perfect day,
    but just leaves you waiting for something
more, always an insatiable woman

        nothing worse than an insatiable woman!
    masturbating over giving footjobs under tables,
over past touching that couldn't even fill me

        it is lonely to exist now but it would
        be maybe not so lonely
        if something had been different
I couldn't pinpoint where something changed within me
    some great shame
        I am self aware enough to
    feel ironic when I let everything go to ruin

when I tell you I want you, I mean my body wants what
    it wants
        and I don't control her!
    would love to be held in one place
would love for my body to be a bed,
    I would love to be a comfort to you

difficult to work through my emotions

I stopped being a bimbo,
        it's not that I don't agree with bimboism
                ideologically;

it's just I want no one to know me,
I do not want to be seen by others
           I will wear my bimbo skin
           for the men when they salivate—
       I will let the demons take a part of what is left
       of this physical form bit by bit but
           I will take off my dumb slut clothes
           and wash off the cum
       I don't need to be empowered,
I just need to have rent paid

       archives of my lust
in other people's text messages,

       how many nudes can you send one person
       before it's a common law marriage?

Are you the Hornet or the Mantis?

mesmerized watching a praying mantis
trap and eat the head off of a murder hornet,
took screenshot of the most intense moments
wanted to text you "look it's u & me!"

brutal giving
the truth is hard to take and I am spiraling in my kitchen
as the world goes by so quickly! how much to be alive right now
and not even to be in a tragic love

infatuation loves to follow me and guide me
through shame depths
you thought the mariana trench
was deep?
wait till you try to get to the bottom of my
love!
I don't know what the end of things look like
but I do know that I have dreamed of fields

where maybe I find myself
somewhere off
wandering aimlessly

xoxo, Gretta

"they say he has a scat fetish,
he goes to the other dungeon"
                    "oh yeah?"

I believe it now, you're a real piece of shit
wooden hangers flying at heads, audio recorders
in the smoking room, a mirror that can be seen through
like the voyeuristic little shit you are

                    you couldn't afford to say no to $220 to keep
                    your employees safe
                    couldn't afford to turn on the air conditioning,
                    the heater unless some ugly john complained

the man who wore sunglasses the whole time, the enema man
who just wanted to have somebody to talk to, the pussy john (PJ)
predator who you pimped every new girl out to

                    I have never wished ill on another human being until
your ugly ass came into my life   you look like some sideline mobster
who gets killed off halfway through the movie, and you probably are
yet somehow you are still alive?
          I mostly just want to push your face into
a pile of shit   I mostly want to whip your back until you can't see
          straight
                    when you let the man beat me and I took off for a week
                    so my body could recover, you pretended to not know
                    it had happened to my face
                    I want to hit your face with

the spiked paddle
                              I want you to feel so much pain
when I saw you in midtown three weeks ago, I glared you down
                              you glared me down
we are in some sort of sick duel,
you can't kill
          what's already long dead
I love a world where the disgusting couch from the cross dressing
room
     is pushed off into the concrete traffic, with you on it!
     I long for a world where every abusive boss is
     sliced! I will not miss you, V!
               I wish you every ill,
     from food poisoning to death by rats

nobody fucks anymore

I vomited in a warehouse bathroom last night,
things are getting a little out of hand!

funny to allow myself into situations that I know
are bad for me and yet do them anyway,

      I'm a maniac baby!
      the apartment bell doesn't ring for me either

      what does one do with uncentered lust?
      I used to think of sex as the moments that mattered,

          everyone wanted to fuck! I did too!
now,
      I feel the need to bring up that I'm a major case
      I feel it within me!
          I wish things were a little different
    but it's all just my inner root, my own hedonism!

      I only want to be touched if you're down to touch me
         again and again

      it's an obsession, like smoking a spliff every hour and
        a   half

I'm a simple woman, I only want to be adored! it's really that easy!

as I wait at the burger joint in chelsea for the friend of a man whose life

I ruined,

I think "I love fall in the city"

a slut in the same old cycle

it has been a minute since I've been played the
fool so expertly you swiftly move over me all
encompassing love bombing as a love language
you were all giving in all the ways that melt
me   and you love to lie
                         you lie to my face
                         I am just a hot young thing
you say you haven't done this before
             when you lie to me like love
when you tell me bullshit
I eat it up the fantasies the delusion when you
             sabotage my space with
Brooklyn Public Library steps, 3:30 pm see u there if i see u

             I walk with the pace of an idiot whose
uterus screams as her IUD wound (she fucked it out of place)
             irritates with every step hurried step to know
to understand better what has overtaken me ruined me fascinated
   me beyond all better judgment
                 and yet again a narcissistic man
                         who has known me a month yet
                              risks everything
      has taken over my mind

             I am removing the parasite now, goodbye!

the balcony I became addicted to nicotine

redefining the boxes I have been put in

      the traffic from the highway sounds exactly like the
      call of the beluga whale

there are birds talking above my head
and there is love in my heart greater
than anyone who has ever hurt me

          I have been made small many times
          it's incredible that my body still exists
          after all I have put it through

              my body is the only thing I will have forever
              and it must hate me
              I am in a complicated relationship with my body,
              send tweet

there is an ambulance roaring outside
for a very fiery second
and there is smoke over the mountain peaks
that I will never touch

twenty-four gone

I love my government mandated walk
every day
   the rich man I am trying to seduce
   for financial security
   lectures me about not isolating enough,
the rich love their "investments"

  today I wanted to perish!
sobbing brutally on my bedroom floor
    I'm the olympic gold medalist of moving
  my bed into the middle of the room so I can
  charge my phone and lay in bed at the same time

I miss my fun sexy life I had just begun to live,
    people keep saying it'll never go back to "normal"
after this
    and they're right

it's been difficult to accept I will never share a joint with
my friends again or snort k in a tiny bathroom with several
bodies and noses and hands and touching so much touching
  I miss touching my friends' faces more than I would
miss being alive but alas we live or we perish, it's all brief anyway!
  my brain has been on fire conversations conversations
voices about death rates and sirens in the distance the fire station
is right   over there but the fire chief died
  I think? so many twitter notifications of loss
obituaries are all the rage right now!

        the nyc health department texts
that we should all be jacking off
        I miss affection! I miss intimacy! I miss the subway
even, it's odd to think I will never eye flirt with someone
at myrtle-wyckoff again and I feel very sad over the loss
of time and of youth and of romance
        but even more sad over the horizontal question marks,
we are all just alive so briefly

everyone digs their way out on their own

so very sorry to leave you there in the pit hole
      void that we all must learn to crawl out of
I never knew a trap was set, the play was written
      long before I ever left!

      forever guilty over choosing myself,
letting go
    of you
          incomparable loss to have found
          myself on the other side of the world
            without you

breaking open my head to make you laugh;
      take anything you need, any knowledge, any love
        any care, any tools, please take it all from me!
          to get out get out get out get out get out,
I know home is never fun
        we could meet somewhere in the middle
  and talk,
      let's just talk
I need you to hear me howl apologies, I need a true intimacy
      with you, I can't go on without you, I can't become
without you,
      safely here with me

  I can't remember the last time I touched your hand

time's little bitch

I call reality "brutal" and time laughs at me
for believing in another option—

       time calls me a little bitch,
       nothing shocks me anymore!

  time is right, I am a little bitch
  with nowhere to go!

        funny how
        we all expect
        certain realities
        and how often
        we find ourselves
        correct

is it
a victim complex?

           is it some sort of joke?

bid you adieu, and you adieu, and you!
I will miss you

no revolution without whore revolution

it's so vulnerable to be myself
    practiced at playing my most sinful
        disgusting and grim
        self for the men with their
        slimey souls and hard rods

                when it snows in the room
                it is sticky in the carpet
                on the tile in the air

I am just a woman who barely knows
    how to walk but I know how
        to talk real good
        make you feel real good
        everyone knows this
        they say it too

        walking through fort greene park
causing chaos if only to amuse myself
        the man asks
"are you familiar with leftism?"
            "baby, I'm a leftist but I organize
            with whores"
crickets
        they don't actually like whores
        they like
        talking points
        but not so much
        us talking

trust issues

obsession with having my cake
and eating it too
                  if I fed it to you
                  would you eat it?
would you let me fit a whole slice
in your mouth, crumbs falling out of your
        mouth
                  do you trust me to feed you?
everything
and anything can be a trust exercise when you have
        trust issues
                I almost bought a second plant
                at the store even though I had
                a cutting in my bag
                that could barely survive next
                to the red velvet slice
                and jar of extra chunky peanut butter
      but I didn't buy the plant
thinking about my hair on fire in a
beautiful woman's bathroom because
I am a sucker for women who follow me
around the apartment with an anal hook
"by the way, I think you forgot this"
                  how could I forget the anal hook
     as I go to smoke a cigarette on the fire
     escape
but the thing is I was on fire and I didn't want
to escape, I just wanted her hands to
                comb the ash from my hair

calling the operator at timber lanes in 2002

update from incest child number two
        I am but a robot of my former self
hello operator I must make a direct call to heaven
        beep beep beep
                                help father I have sinned
        Father ?

                FATHER!

it's funny for you to give the silent treatment
                                        weren't always so
                                                silent were you?
what happens when baby puts YOU in the corner!

Hello Operator, r u still there? I don't know what else to say
        but your presence is comforting

when people die they're usually dead so it's cool how
        you're still alive but killed by choice every single
                day in my heart
        I sob asking heaven if you are redeemable
they text back: lol nah sorry babe

I understand you don't want me baby but what do I do?

insatiable on a long leash,
the pup humping your leg
I just want to fuck and be fucked,
right now!
do you understand
what I mean?
maybe it's my avoidance issues,
been avoiding the slaa meeting

I love throwing myself at people who
point me always in other directions
go seek, go find!
well, what if what I find
is just
solitude?
what I have always known and been haunted
by?

incredible how easy it is to lose me

brutal! unforgiving! demanding!

ales tells me I deserve what I want but what I want
is something unattainable: a security blanket in myself,
grounded in myself, to not feel bonkers
all the time!   the other night when the man handed
me the envelope I went into the bathroom, he talked
through the door

I pushed him onto a cloud where we stayed for a moment
            I want to be loved in the fantasy by someone who
                    knows the real me,
not my fake name or my projected internet visage
but someone who knows how I am when
I am my most small
not powerful at all
but you can't
find that
easily

                            there is the public face
                                    but my private face
                                        is ugly,
                    brutal, unforgiving, demanding!
                                    the public eye is a trap,
                                    there is no growth there

        you say I am evocative
                with no explanation

a fucking fantasy

holding the space between us, the thick air
when eyes meet with a knowing
            rare to undress oneself in one's actions
                        the public turmoil
                        of hands touching
                        barely
                        resting on shoulders
                        the lean against
before love becomes demanding
a taking operation / / how does one bottle
            the feeling of when you barely know
                        someone but you want
                                    to feel their face
                                                against yours

            lover, each one is
            a fucking fantasy

what is worse
            to love each other out of one another's lives
or to wake up one morning and not feel
the thick air but instead an air of vacancy
                        a standard emotional reality
                                    that can not be contained
                                                manipulated nor
                                                            copied

I beg to be devoured before flying

apologize for the disappearing act
it's easy to JUMP when directed
problems arise when every light
is emerald green in the sky
on the street
in the eyes of the one you
love
so I jump baby,
and I always land exactly as I land
bruised battered body rather be buttered up
and baked, guzzled down into your belly
yet instead eternal focus all signs
point to bottomless loss!
sorry babe I couldn't
really understand love
before I met you either,
all I know is that some
women are too crazy
to be loved or so they
tell me time and time
again
sexy body as a little bomb

Tick
Tock
Tick
Tock
Tick
Tock

this feeling will never end! I bid you adieu!
I love you but goodbye, I'm insatiable
honey! favors come in all shapes
and sizes

the end

have a bad habit (many bad habits)
    of hatching my heart
    before it even warms

        I'm trying to not count you
        until you hatch,
    having been the disappointed woman before
    I know it's not a good look on me!

the silliness of youth is not realizing how quickly
    ten years goes by and then another
        until you are past half a century
          and your legs won't let
            you GO
    like they used to!
          your daughter, she
          stops calling but the years
          continue onward,
    the radio show
    blares out
          "THE END OF SOCIETY AS WE KNOW
              IT!"

you knew this day would come wrapped in fear
    sitting at your little desk bed table
    that you have, only to find that
        there is nothing you can do to change
          a cement brick

regrettable french man

do I talk a big talk?
    walk a big game?

we fuck in the way I like,
        loveless with respect
        the view from the window
        out of your apartment is wealthy

I see the little joggers on the street below,
as you raw me like the little slut I
        so want to be

                I wish that it was easier
                to be one of those women
                who go to yoga twice a week,
                content with their brunch buddies,
                and long term boyfriend that
                thinks sexting online isn't cheating

I should have fed you cake but instead I dropped it
        on the floor, made you clean up the homemade
            ice cream
                    I leave after cuddling for five minutes
                    you can hold my feet but that's
                    not love, baby

Olympic Gold Medalist in Fucking, Trained From Birth

men wanted virgin and whore at the same time,
so I became both

        male desire perverted,
        child glaring at her father
        all men until eventually,
    the words aren't as scary

    the faces change until flashback
    emotionally unhinged in bed,
       I'm a sex god baby!

MALE DESIRE MOLDED ME UNTIL ALL THAT
WAS LEFT WAS DESIRE

    and it wasn't even mine

cremated not stirred

it sucks when men talk and you can no longer
fuck them
                    certain realities deserve to be kept
at a distance—
fantasy!
            certain loves you fly too close
                    to holiness
                            I have turned to ash
                            many times over
                                    how
                                    many
                                    have
                                    thrown
                                    what
                                    is
                                    left
                                    of
                                    me
                                    into the sea?

garden shears will do if it's all you have

connected eternally by the root that
grabs at my ankles with every step,
the same roots that guide yours
        we practice sword-making
        polish every day
        until we slowly
        saw   them   off

liberation only comes to those aware
        they are controlled

                the man who kicked dogs, threw
        forks, curses under his breath at the
slight change in the air, perverted

he is only a boogeyman to us now!

obsession with domestication

        a desert vacation to fuck smoke
touch I want to write a novel during our love
so every time I read it I can't help but think of
the time you made me cry over something
unimportant or fucking in unique places
in a home
                I want to be domestic with you
let's have a spat, plead forgiveness, spoil me
        all-giving siren
                      on the way to pussy heaven
      it's necessary to love where the clouds
are pink

Goodbye to Jack who never got a chance to be a good dog

everything breaks
bites fights back
eventually

put down
for bad behavior
we are all reflections of our
environments
when
locked in the bathroom you piss on the floor
they ask why did you piss
on the floor?
the wild streets aren't free to roam
for a dog like you
but they are for a dog like me

I wish we could have went on
long walks
together
on the beach
in a warm place
liberating myself alone
was a mistake

we all bring what we bring

never feel "good" enough for monogamy
                    when I run out to see you it is
                    sporadic purposeful planned chaos

     being together is better than winning one hundred
     tickets at the bowling alley arcade,
                            besides if I did
     win one hundred tickets I would buy you a stuffed
     animal that looks more cartoonish than real
     that you can hold when you don't feel real

                    we can have an unreality together
              the pink sky that has been on fire
        will light our way
to wherever we end up going

liu wei

in my head I am on a beach in malta
we are juiced out on nebbiolo wine,
direct sunlight, laughter

I have ate every little cake
enjoyed every little pleasure
even those, especially those,
not meant for me

when we are together life is
not mine, I am someone else
no longer the walking shame but
instead a pride

when we are together I am your
american poet daughter that
jet sets to edinburgh, rome,
shanghai, the ends of the earth
to be as you see me

years ago after four sleepless hong
kong nights, the hangzhou guest bedroom
a note in the morning
"sunshine, off to the grocery, be back
by noon"

what I used to fear

loud voices
cursing under jaw
dying alone (now I know we all do)
a joint bank account

baby birding fantasy

eating day old chips
want to be baby birded
                by you

redefining intimacy by checking
the citizen surveillance to watch
the police chase happening three
blocks away from your house

            you keep your heart locked
            surrounded by moat
                    but I can find a way

                    I am terrifyingly determined
                        to love

kathy acker where are you?

I haven't responded and have no intention
to,
      send receive send receive
all communication is now
      a few dots of forever
      connecting us

I think of my mother kathy acker
      and my left breast
I think of my mother kathy acker
      and think of the sex show
      I've been starring in from
      the womb,
          I think of mother
      and I am a neglected small thing
but some mothers teach you through their absence
      how to survive

I think of mother I think of mother I think of mother

      all the time

wishful thinking

I believe in our love because what
else is there to believe in ?

blizzards don't stop me from finding
myself at chelsea pier
at a beckoning call
a subway line straight to you
a swift movement
of my heart
meeting my body halfway
across the city where you
are always
the sky is grey
and mutating under frost
I got in my head, baby, I thought I
was evil! you holding my hand
guiding me out of the grim
through the snow
I want to know you
in so many contexts, at every hour
including the witching
I want to sync up with you
in a way that is safe!
I love looking at you because you're
right there,
taking a photo of the frying pan
in the hudson

dead girls 100% off

my malware is special, the phishing is precious!
they always said whatever you post on the internet
        is forever,
                    my data will
        live long past me
my ad space will exist long past me

(unhinged brunette shoegaze dogs adopt dogs
queer cinema white 25 mid-twenties vacation
vacation jobs are looking to hire you now spicy
burritos in 5 mile distance mid-century furniture
amrrak 40% off to anywhere you want to be)

        they advertise to dead bodies
        to unviewed screens,
            they say you can't take it with you

go argue somewhere else

           performing the same old aesthetics
feels violent, I don't give a shit about your take, baby

        I want, I have never feigned I don't
                I will be far away soon enough
                not enough waterfalls lately
                I have been so stuck
                forgot that if I am unwanted
                            I can go elsewhere !

        I don't want to go elsewhere, little body
        small in a corner I now miss
to be there, to be nothing, to be unreachable
                I don't want to interact with your
                world,
        I barely know my own world
                        fucking is a portal, desire is
                        nowhere to be found simply
                        liberation from a moment
                        yet you open your eyes
                        STILL HERE!

I understand the enema man now, I get it

excavated myself far enough
                            an emotional enema
                I've been cleared through
            everyone knows my inner heart
        how my mother's voice sounds
how my father's rage goes

                    time to build
                        again

unavoidable grief

corona whiplash!
listening to the snow melt,
distanced disaster
I cannot save you anymore
or maybe ever,
dominos pushed by someone
more powerful
having been small my whole life—
barely walking
away from Walnut Avenue
the children are coughing!

revenge comes to those who fester

being liked is the least of my worries, but thank you
for reminding me
        I have googled the same name twenty
        times in two years to the same result!
                some would set an alert,
        I like to purposefully dwell in my deep dives
                revenge is hotter than sex but it's evil
                to admit,
        what if my little body daydreams of you
        slipping on ice,
                it's so sexy when karma does you in
    I'm praying for you,
                        that we will never run into each other
    I'm praying for myself,
to have the strength if we do

collapsed on us, didn't it?

the before times
the kissing times
the "yeah let's just meet in Chelsea" times
                    a whole collapsed
                    existence gone
                    I didn't even touch
                                        everything
                                        I wanted to
spent nearly a year inside a sex dungeon
        only to find myself indoors
                            I crave big windows
                                    big fucking
                                    big desires

        in other places they're already fucking
        strangers without regard
                            I get nervous
                            in the grocery
                            store,
                    I grab the french bread pizzas
            and nothing else

guarded feminine

vomiting out lately
                to anyone who will listen
                except the precious inclinations
                that I barely understand
                                cannot share what I do not know
      so I'm sorry if I seem distant, baby
    looking at you
    I want to understand
    how you look at someone
    else
                    am I just entertainment
        in your stop here
                                having been in unrequited love
                                many times, this isn't it but where
                                ever I have found you stomping
                                around inside my thoughts
                                I still cannot read you

    men are easy
    they want from you the moment you say hello
                    it is easy to rest into the void
                        with them
                                to misalign myself
                                in order to feel nothing

I want everything in the small nothing of you

I have your name

THE WOMAN TWEETS THAT SHE BEAT THE MAN
WHO GROPED HER AND IT WAS GLORIOUS
      I WANT TO ASK SO BADLY "HOW DID IT FEEL
            TO LET INTO HIM
               TO FEEL IT ALL UNTIL HE WAS
         BUT A PULP UNDER YOU?"
I HOLD BACK BUT
I STILL WOULD LIKE TO KNOW

new definitions of old experiences

lost my designer thong in the daylight of your room
      happy president's day, it's hot when you pull out
      onto my chest before I call the car
      pulling me into your bedroom
      as I get dressed
      to fuck me
      one last time
                  we are creating a new definition of
                  "fucking" all fuckers do in their
                  own way but there will never be another
           me fucking another you

how to redirect fate

broken world molding us
progress
recall momma drinking a cocktail
at the applebees, tears
my momma
tells me it feels like all went to
hell in a handbasket
how to change circumstance
beyond control
the minor feudalism of being a woman
without capital
witnessed
my sister
provide
home
babies
bread
to
an
outline
momma
is
working
every
day
with
a
mask
on

no future to write to but people need poetry now

climate crisis forever
every poem written is for
a dead and dying world

       collapse
       under the weight of
       life ephemera
ambulance orchestra
       extinct bird symphony
    the sounds you make when we are
shoreline french kisses iceberg
                 till melt
       if you and I
       get washed in the sea
       let's meet
       where
       there
       is
       no shore

I Want a Family Free Feminism Where We all Fuck in the End

if there is a feminism I want it to be a feminism that protects the earth I want it to be a feminism that fucks around I want it to be a feminism that is beyond the Sex Question, and onto the Cumming Question: when will I cum, can I cum, do I cum, when will I next cum, is there such a thing as too much cumming, sometimes certainly not enough cumming I don't want a feminism that is without whores, cunts, cumming, gossip, dykes, fags, the deconstruction of all that exists right now, I want to destroy the Iphone, I want to Destroy the American Dream within Me, Within You, Within Us I think there is something extremely fucked up about childhood, nothing more perverse than a family

all of memory is a graveyard, if you think about it

                        is there any
            escape   available
I used to   speed by
but I haven't   been able to
        go anywhere   fast lately but I day
                  dream of   forever like
                        maybe
                              liberation and pause
                              come simultaneously
                              all of life merely a
                              second coming of your
                              inner child
                  feel as if I am fading
                  in the memory of
                  everyone who
                  has ever loved me
                                          saying goodbye
                              in my own time
                        but being forgotten
                  in theirs

body alone, body here, body where

untethered, made of sheer spite
                      I sometimes walk down a
                      street incredibly aware that
                      my body stands alone,

       my mother is not waiting behind
       the corner
my father is a ghost
                         my sisters,
                where have my sisters been
                as I've been away?
as my body
has let go
of everything!
                      sobbing to disco in a bedroom
                      that no one visits
                              body bound to place
          I wanted to be away for so long I only knew how
          to be away and then there was no way to go back
          no one ever tells you that back is non existent
          there is only the cold devastating future

'free falling' by tom petty

I have been wrung out
yet still unleash more
        is there any end to want
        to tormented grief, labor,
        overdraft fees, banks, loans,
        the debt clock is ticking
        there is so little between me
        and falling through the earth

distraction? thanks!

I like when you stop
my dressing
pull down panties
fill me
against your bed
sweater hanging
off arm
I am but a receiver
of power cum pleasure

trapeze crash

acrobatic heart, expertise is breaking!
vulnerability is a half-cracked egg
I don't blame you for the void, I have
parents for that

or maybe I don't!

jennicam

she says it's totally different
to sound someone when
you're in love

      pussies founding businesses,
      pussies as a business

I cried listening to jennicam talk
about a client not feeling alone
on a saturday doing laundry
because she was alone on a
saturday night doing laundry

it's called being a dream maker,
             honey!
      not everyone has the moxy
to live a life of devotion

billboard memoriam nudes

there is the big overlooking bad on the horizon
above everything else
the dark scary that is whispered about or yelled about
or casually mentioned in so many words and phrases
global warming climate change late capitalism
anthropocene extinction co2 levels flooding starvation
extremity
      and the words in the beginning were small
or maybe I was small

      a child on the brink of it all
      coming of age in the last age
      the final age of humans

I became in the era of the Internet
              post-9/11
         Facebook Twitter Brands
      Corporatism and Surveillance
my whole life is an archive online
      on the Cloud
      every thought is known every nude
      stored on the Cloud somewhere
      in the end of all things my body
      will exist formless in the Cloud
please do not delete my Selfies when I am dead,
      instead use them on billboards
      this is my wish

RIP The Free Internet

I love the little pieces of me
that only exist online
never archived, never catalogued,
lost to the graveyard of the internet,
Home of My Youth!
my sweet sweet youth
before the planet heated,
before I could comprehend loss

the spring of the Web,
the golden green years of surfing
the cyber!
people reaching through the nether,
another frontier
and yet the frontier conquered
by corporate demons
vocal recognition,
THIS AD IS SPONSORED BY
YOUR INNERMOST DESIRE!

my sweet sweet
loss of innocence
in cyber chat rooms,
perpetually reaching to the void
for affection

it's not illegal to do this   xoxo gossip poet

did I cry too much baby

sobbing watching sleepless in seattle
                next to you
                                holding you
                                forward
                                tipping
                                red wine
                                into your mouth
        when you touch
        me, no one else has touched me before!

                fucking up the hash browns, you politely eat
I wish
time wasn't a factor
        in everything,
                        companionship should come easy
                but am flushed with how
        easy it is with those who are already gone

not wiping the oil off my glasses because I know
        it's from when you kissed me

someone save me from my own cycles

birthing history moments in time that just pass so quickly by
        and here we are you and i just figuring out time on this rock
that is just like many other rocks except here we are and i wonder
if there will be another time just like this again where the light hits
your face perfectly in the afternoon, safety comes to very few and
only sparse i think that if you were to have met me a few years ago
you would have found me dirty and fucked me and left but here we
are i wonder if you and i will ever go somewhere else other than
        here

i felt my body differently when i was near you every space between us
is a loving tense absence what can i say if you touch me i will melt into
you and lose myself until you can barely see me until i barely see me
i have tried to find a solution to the problem
hammer   open your bedroom wall,
stick me in

no that will never work but i can be good for many things
not just baths when i let the luxury watch dealer piss on me golden
hot steam in the marriott in hoboken
(the same one you know who did you know what at,
river reflection last looks on planet earth),

i prayed, degradation baptism where every shame falls off me
down the   drain

flashback time travel machine

slapped the tourist across the face and he came
      in his pants
                    wiped down in the bathroom
               he told me that nyc was dirty

exited this timeline
                 into another
         digital eighteen-year-old slut
              sexting voids
                 grabbing at
              digital physicality
              safe sex is when no
              one can touch me
              and I choose all the angles
I haven't beat my pain slut
      in a year
              when we first met, kismet
              had to scrub blood off the floors

walking down fifth avenue
         a cop followed us for two blocks
         saying goodbye at the subway
         the cop loses interest
              I light a cigarette
              call simone
              next to the church
              as suits walk by
              and in front and behind

hear me say
          "he was right behind
          me, like baby he could
have stepped on me, we literally
weren't even sessioning
he's a massage therapist, he straight
up moved my muscles, but that's besides
the point, it's like he could smell it on me, you know? he left
          another cop to follow me"
CLICK

     this timeline frightens me onto the next
               it has been so long since I visited you
               the jacaranda blossoms of youth have
               long died
                         no longer children drinking
                         our weight
                                   in cornershop
                                   beer
no longer hurting each other just to prove we can
                         this timeline has ended
          in a different world
               the girl who cleaned everything
               screams "PIGS, I'M GETTING THE
                    FUCK OUT OF HERE"
               blue vests times eight in the elevator
               camera
          body shaking as I count condoms on me
                         cops got off at the food
                                   court
                         false alarm
               body shake

     body shake

I daydream of daisies pushing
upwards
fields, fresh grapes, coconut water,
the waters of adolescence so warm to swim
naked in the embryo of my life

your JSTOR hat when you are drunk at 2pm

no one is innocent
everyone harms
one another,
no reality unscraped by another
      we mutate next to one
      another, every interaction
      rubs off onto me

      I want to have your   against me
            weight

you drove me cuckoo
down under
      implanted some insecurities
      was it within you all along,
      this evil growth?
  i
  have
  returned
  from
  burying
  myself!
        some loves can only blow
          up, darling!
     you were my favorite
        terrorist (of my reality)
        "the king of gaslighting" is

what your "crazy ex"
later called you

i listened to hand habits 'placeholder' for a week straight

my heart, otherwise known as the grief of You
      building together combining lives becoming
      Together until   we weren't
          I ran
   from
you
         I didn't mean to
         disappear
     but the room had such little
     light through the courtyard
   and prospect called
           I stayed away   as I know how
        to do
     and
I don't know how to get back to you

           your absence
              felt
              like
              i
              had
              lost
              myself
but that's why I had to go, baby

     when the police helicopters almost
        crashed into crowds and
        the philosopher raped me in

my friend's apartment
I wanted to call you and tell you
because I want you to know everything
about me still but I didn't
and when you text me about tony soprano six months
later
I sob in the kitchen
I don't know how to go back   I don't know how to return
I don't know if one should return
if I can
I miss you all the time

fondue for two

        friday night sobbing in the uber
that you bought me
it is good to feel pain, to be alive, to know
that I can still cry over something that has
nothing to do with death, the ice melting,
the ice generally, aj, addy, mrs walker, bisma,
dj, sam, names that have disappeared and reappear
at their choosing
                it is good to cry over wanting something
                      instead of at my gaping loss
                      my family, my past selves that
                      no one but me will ever know
    it is good to want
    even if it is painful
                    desire is a rage
                          time is a bubble bursting
          these are the
          parts of me I find ugly
      they are salted and carameled and poured
over with cheese and chocolate, I want to nourish you
                open up !

close 2 u

do i eat u up i am sorry

                for enjoying
                a delicious meal
                courtesy of what
                you have provided

but i just want to be
close 2 u, i feel pathetic

                 maybe I just don't
                 have it in me
                       but
                 my heart
                 in the body
                 bag kicked

            by my own
                  desire

    I just wanted to
        Get   Off   and Feel   Good
           but feel Loved

                       too
    it's okay cowboy, I recognize when
    the rodeo is up, I have been the clown
    many a time

apologizing for feeling

heart race back forth

        she   does

a   flip

look   at

her   go

      like a dove

             in the desert night

        I wanted to get used up

        be used up

              some defining narrative

              of self degradation in lieu (of)

              love never stood a chance

     you fucked me   like

     a bitch in heat

                 is my love a horror show?

            terrifying to make promises to me,

      I could fly off the handle baby!

disappearance as foreplay

           I felt I'd been good

             I didn't go nuts but I apologized

                  anyway

     dancing on my grave baby

     dancing on my grave

     dancing on my

     dancing on

     dancing

        into the desert night

on the day of

there's something about when violence finds you
       like a gust of ominous future

       the past is simply what it is, brutal
I seem to give it all but it is a trick of the eye
what appears depth is void a nothingness
            my emotional center is so far from here
            lost
            in
            the graveyard of childhood

       on the day after everything, nothing else
                               happened
   or did it?

looking for a daddy

I want to go into a bodega and buy one hundred
packs of cigarettes, I want to carry them all in a little
bag and smoke them one by one as I walk wherever
my little legs go
        I wonder eventually if I will walk into you or maybe
        right past you and isn't it so typical to run straight
        past or besides without looking, like you are on the
        street and we run past each other at the speed of
        our days
                would I, will I
                run away
I've gotten really good at one step in front of the other
        at adapting my body to new places and faces
Always On The Go!
            I know the shame isn't in me now
            yet the aftertaste hits hard
            I question everything I have ever
            known before noon,
            by three pm I am drunk
            and dipping my toes in distraction
            of the same old variety that never
            steers me wrong until I am but a
            weeping woman wanting
            more

Acknowledgements

There are so many people who made *Bimboland* possible. It feels nearly impossible to express that I never thought this book was possible, so I would like to first thank Nicodemus Nicoludis and Chris Molnar for giving my poetry a home. I'd like to thank my editor and friend Simone Wolffe for editing *Bimboland*, this book wouldn't have been possible without you, and similarly, I wouldn't be who I am without you. Now in no specific order of appearance: I'd like to thank Erin Violet Taylor for friending me on Facebook when we were teens and for endlessly supporting me and seeing me. I'd like to thank Nurul-Hannah Azura Seddon for everything, you changed me eternally. Stacey Teague, Rory Green, and Rosie Power, thank you for your friendships from Sydney to Hong Kong to Tulsa. Thank you to Liam Tay-Kearney and Alex Kirk for loving me when I didn't know how to love myself, we will always have Hangzhou. Johntom Knight, we got out, go us. I'm proud of you, thank you for always seeing my vision, however small or large. Xochitl Deseret and Livia Thayer, thank you for growing up with me, I love you both. Rachel Phelps, I could write a whole book of thanks for you, I love you, I love you, from Timberlanes to the grave. Thank you to my Mom, for bottomless love. Thank you to Danielle and Kelley for always loving me as I am, and my love to Jorge, Lucas, and Molly Anne.

Thank you to Liu Wei, for being my friend and always reminding me of the way forward. You changed my life, taught me so much, and allowed me space to heal in our friendship. Forever. Thank you Tony Tulathimutte for being my first friend in New York and for supporting me through one of the hardest periods of my life with grace, ease, and care. Thank you to Ed Ongweso for being my friend. Thank you to Molly Soda for introducing me to American Spirits Light Blue. Thank you to Matt Fennell for going to the movies with me. Thank you to Lanna Tenney, Maya Bensalem, Dakota Delvalle, and Briana Rodriguez for everything. Thank you Shelby Lorman and Aiden Arata. Thank you to Rosemary Donahue for teaching me how to write a pitch. Thank you to the girls at the den. Thank you to Grace. Thank you to the lady who used to run the banh mi shop on 8th avenue in Sunset Park. I wish your restaurant hadn't closed down. Thank you to Nadine Smith and Etan Weisfogel for letting me into your lives with love and acceptance. Thank you to Soenke, Marcelle, Nigel, Lorna, Adel and Jocelyn for always encouraging me in my learning. Thank you to all the poets I know, who are all deserving of thanks and love for keeping poetry alive and breathing constantly. Thank you to all the whores I love. Thanks to god, if you exist.

MORE FROM ARCHWAY EDITIONS

Ishmael Reed – *The Haunting of Lin-Manuel Miranda*
Unpublishable (edited by Chris Molnar and Etan Nechin)
Gabriel Kruis – *Acid Virga*
NDA: An Autofiction Anthology (edited by Caitlin Forst)
Mike Sacks – *Randy*
Mike Sacks – *Stinker Lets Loose*
Paul Schrader – *First Reformed*
Archways 1 (edited by Chris Molnar and Nicodemus Nicoludis)
Brantly Martin – *Highway B: Horrorfest*
Stacy Szymaszek – *Famous Hermits*
cokemachineglow (edited by Clayton Purdom)
Ishmael Reed – *Life Among the Aryans*
Alice Notley – *Runes and Chords*

Archway Editions can be found at your local bookstore or ordered directly through Simon & Schuster.

Questions? Comments? Concerns? Send correspondence to:

Archway Editions
c/o powerHouse Books
220 36th St., Building #2
Brooklyn, NY
11232